Rosa Parks

FREEDOM RIDER

Rosa Parks
FREEDOM RIDER

By Keith Brandt and Joanne Mattern
Illustrated by Gershom Griffith

SCHOLASTIC INC.

New York   Toronto   London   Auckland   Sydney
Mexico City   New Delhi   Hong Kong   Buenos Aires

ISBN-13: 978-0-439-66045-7
ISBN-10: 0-439-66045-9

12 11 10 9 8 7 6   9 10 11/0

Printed in the U.S.A.   23

First printing, January 2006

CONTENTS

CHAPTER 1:
A Seat on the Bus

It was early in the evening of December 1, 1955. Rosa Parks finished work at the Montgomery Fair department store and caught a bus to go home. She was tired after a long day of sewing in the store's tailor shop.

Rosa paid her fare, found an empty seat in the eleventh row, and sat down. She could not sit in the first ten rows, because those seats were only for white passengers. The bus soon filled up. The black people sat in the back and the white people sat in the front. In those days, black and white people were often separated that way in the American South. This separation is called racial segregation. It was the law, and in Montgomery, Alabama, this kind of law was strictly enforced.

Rosa sat in the middle of the bus. It was all right for blacks to sit there if no white person had to stand. But on that evening, as more passengers boarded the bus, a white man was left without a seat. The driver told Rosa and the three other black people in her row to get up and move to the back of the bus. The others followed his orders. Rosa stayed in her seat.

The driver stood and walked back to where Rosa was sitting. "Are you going to stand up and move to the back?" he asked her.

"No," she said calmly. "Why should I have to get up and stand?"

"Well, I'm going to have you arrested," the driver said.

"You may do that," Rosa answered.

The driver left the bus and called the police. Rosa didn't move. Two policemen arrived and asked her why she didn't move to the back of the bus. Rosa

responded with a question of her own. "Why do you all push us around?" she asked.

One of the officers answered, "The law is the law and you're under arrest."

Rosa was placed in the back of the police car and taken to jail. There she was fingerprinted and put in a cell—all because she refused to give up her seat on a public bus.

Later, Rosa was asked why she had refused to give up her seat. After all, she had been following the rules of segregation all of her life. Rosa said, "I had had enough. I wanted to be treated like a human being. I knew someone had to take the first step, and I made up my mind not to move."

Word of Rosa's arrest spread quickly. Three of her friends arrived at the jail to arrange for her release. They were Clifford and Virginia Durr, and Edgar D. Nixon. Mr. and Mrs. Durr were white. He was a lawyer, and they were both active members of the civil-rights movement.

E.D. Nixon, a black man, was regional director of the Brotherhood of Sleeping Car Porters,

the first black trade union in America. He was also president of the Alabama chapter of the National Association for the Advancement of Colored People (NAACP). Rosa was also a member of the NAACP, serving as secretary of the branch in Montgomery, Alabama.

Rosa was allowed to leave with Nixon and the Durrs after her friends posted one hundred dollars for her bail. Raymond Parks had also arrived by then, and he took his wife home. He was very relieved that Rosa was safe. So was Rosa's mother, Leona McCauley. They knew it was dangerous for black people to go against white authority in the South. They both told Rosa to pay the fourteen-dollar fine and end the whole matter.

But the matter was just beginning. When Rosa refused to give up her seat on the bus, she started another American revolution. Rosa decided to challenge the bus segregation law. She talked it over with Mr. Nixon and the Durrs, and they

promised to join in the fight. That night, they agreed on what steps to take.

The first big decision was to refuse to pay the fine. It meant that Rosa might have to go to jail. But she was ready for that.

Her family was not so sure. Ray Parks feared for his wife's safety. He was sure she would be hurt, and maybe even killed. Rosa's mother, who lived with the family, was also worried. But Rosa was so determined to challenge the segregation law that her husband and mother finally agreed.

The next step was to organize the whole black community to boycott the city's buses. (A boycott is when people join together and refuse to buy a product or use a service.) The city of Montgomery earned a large amount of money from bus fares. Most of those fares were paid by black people. The boycott's aim was to make the city lose money if they kept the bus segregation law.

Late on the night of December 1, a group called the Women's Political Council

met. They printed 35,000 copies of a notice that was distributed to blacks all over the city. It read: "This woman's case will come up on Monday, December 5. We are, therefore, asking every Negro to stay off the buses Monday in protest of the arrest and trial. Don't ride the buses to work, to town, to school, or anywhere on Monday. . . . Please, children and grown-ups, don't ride the bus at all on Monday."

Word of the boycott spread during the weekend. Ministers of black churches used their Sunday sermons to talk about the boycott. They praised Rosa's courage. They told every churchgoer to pass the word to friends, relatives,

and neighbors. The church was a central feature of black life in Montgomery. The organizers knew that if church leaders supported the boycott, they would have a good chance to succeed.

CHAPTER 2:
On Our Feet

The boycott on Monday was a huge success. Hardly any black people took a bus that day. Empty bus followed empty bus all around the city. Meanwhile, the sidewalks were packed with black people walking to work and to school. Taxis were also filled with black passengers. One black man was even spotted riding a mule down the street! People did whatever they had to do to support the boycott.

On that same Monday morning, Rosa appeared in court. She was found guilty of breaking the Montgomery segregation law. She refused to pay the fourteen-dollar fine. Instead, her lawyer filed an appeal. This meant that the case had to be heard by a higher court. Only a higher court could actually change the segregation law.

When Rosa and her lawyer left the courtroom, they were stunned to see a crowd of about five hundred black people standing silently on the

sidewalk and the courthouse steps. When they saw Rosa, they greeted her with cheers and applause.

Rosa was thrilled. Tears came to her eyes as she realized she was not alone in this fight. For the first time in her memory, the black community was openly united. At that moment, Rosa knew she had done the right thing. She also knew there was a lot more that needed to be done.

That night, there was a meeting at the Holt Street Baptist Church. The church had been chosen as the site of the meeting because it

could hold 1,000 people. The organizers weren't sure how many people would show up. They knew that the black citizens of Montgomery had walked miles that day to support the boycott, and everybody was exhausted. But that didn't stop them from coming.

Minute by minute, the church filled until there were no more seats. Hundreds gathered on the church grounds and in the streets surrounding the building. Loudspeakers had to be set up outside to carry the words of the meeting to everyone. It was so crowded that the men who spoke at the meeting had to leave their cars five blocks away from the church and walk through the thick crowd.

The big question to be decided at the meeting was, will the boycott continue? The black people were tired. Some were afraid. The white community was angry. Everyone knew what dangers lay ahead—loss of jobs, arrests, violence . . . maybe even death.

Then a new voice spoke up. It was the twenty-six-year-old minister from the Dexter Avenue Baptist Church. He had lived in Montgomery less than a year, and most of the people in the city did not know much about him. His name was Reverend Martin Luther King, Jr.

King began by speaking about the history of segregation. "There comes a time when people get tired of being trampled over by the iron feet of oppression," he said. ". . . We are here this evening because we're tired now."

He also spoke about the dangers of carrying on a boycott. Then King talked about the need for a boycott, and about the rightness of it, warning that there must be no violence on the part of the black community.

"The only weapon that we have in our hands this evening is the weapon of protest," he said. ". . . And let each of us go out from here resolved . . . to never give back one inch until we shall be accorded the full respect and rights. . . . Right here in Montgomery, when the history books are written in the future, somebody will have to say, 'There lived a race of people, black people . . . who had the moral courage to stand up for their rights.'"

The crowd hung on to Reverend Martin Luther King's every word. When he finished speaking, the crowd cheered for fifteen minutes. Then there was a vote for continuing the boycott. Every man, woman, and child roared approval. The boycott went on!

CHAPTER 3:
Poor, but Proud

Rosa became a symbol because of her brave act. In that way, she was special. But in other ways, she was a typical black American. Her history is the story of many black people in the American South.

Rosa's roots were in Africa. Her ancestors were brought to America by force and put to work as slaves. Slavery ended after the Civil War, but life didn't become much easier for black people.

She was born on February 4, 1913, into a world of segregation and racism. At the time, her family lived in Tuskegee, Alabama, where her father, James McCauley, worked as a carpenter. Soon after Rosa was born, the McCauleys moved to nearby Abbeville, to live with James's family. A few years later, Rosa's parents separated. Rosa did not see her father again until she was grown up.

Mrs. McCauley took Rosa and Rosa's baby brother, Sylvester, to live with her own parents, in Pine Level, Alabama. Then Mrs. McCauley, who was a teacher, went back to work to support herself and her children.

Today, a good teacher like Mrs. McCauley can get a job in any public school. But in those days, a black teacher could only teach black children in separate schools. Black teachers were also paid much less than white teachers.

There was a great difference between education for blacks and whites. White schools were well built and well equipped, and the teachers were well paid. White children had textbooks, heated classrooms, buses, and a full school year.

Black children went to run-down schools
with no heat, no desks, no textbooks, and no school
supplies. They
often had

to walk many miles to school. Also, they went to school only part of every year. The rest of the time, black children were expected to work in the fields, picking cotton, weeding, and doing other farm chores.

Although the system was cruel and unfair, black people had no way to change it. The laws made them second-class citizens and kept them that way. Black people who protested or behaved like free human beings were punished. Sometimes the punishment was the loss of a job or land. Often it was much worse.

CHAPTER 4:
Danger!

All over the South, there were gangs of white people who used violence and murder to control black people. The worst of these groups was the Ku Klux Klan (KKK). Klan members wore white sheets and hoods to hide their identities. They often committed their terrible deeds at night, burning churches and homes, and killing any blacks they found. They were never punished for any of their crimes.

When Mrs. McCauley went back to teaching, her parents, Rose and Sylvester Edwards, took

care of the children. Mr. and Mrs. Edwards owned eighteen acres of land. They grew corn, fruit, yams, and many other vegetables. They raised their own pigs, cows, and chickens, and caught fish in a nearby creek. If they couldn't raise what they needed, they traded for it at the town store.

Though the family was poor, there was always enough to eat. In addition to caring for their farm, Rosa's grandparents also picked cotton, sweet potatoes, corn, and peanuts at a nearby plantation. Rosa joined them when she was only six years old. She earned just one dollar for every one hundred pounds of cotton she picked. When she was older, Rosa earned fifty cents a day chopping cotton. Both jobs were physically demanding. Rosa later recalled the hot ground burning her feet through her shoes.

Despite the hard work, life on the farm for little Rosa and Sylvester was happy and secure. But there was always a cloud that hung over their lives. It was the ever-present danger of the KKK and other racist groups.

One of Rosa's first experiences with racism came when she was five years old. The KKK was very active in her part of Alabama. They rode around at night, destroying black churches, burning crosses on black property, breaking into black homes, and killing the people who lived there. Every night, Mr. Edwards sat in his home with a shotgun close by. If the Klan attacked his house, he would be ready for them.

"I don't know how long I would last if they came breaking in here," he told Rosa. "But I'm getting the first one who comes through the door."

On those nights, Rosa sat on the floor next to her grandfather's rocking chair. He told her stories about his parents and about his mother's difficult life as a slave. He talked about the Civil War, and what happened when Yankee soldiers came and told the slaves they were free.

Rosa loved and admired Grandfather Edwards. He had a very hard life, but he did not let it defeat him. He had an inner strength that was unshakable, and he taught his family not to put up with bad treatment from anyone.

Grandfather Edwards spoke to black and white people with equal dignity and honesty. Everyone knew he expected the same respect from them. It was these qualities that Rosa took for her own. They gave her a solid core of values that stayed with her for the rest of her life. Later, Rosa said that her family gave her the belief that "we should all be equal, whether we had the money or the material goods, that we could be respected and respect other people."

CHAPTER 5:

Going to School

Mrs. McCauley's teaching job kept her away from home all week, but she always spent weekends with her children. During those weekends, she taught Rosa and Sylvester to read and write. Even before Rosa started school, she had a strong love for books and learning.

The school Rosa attended had one room for all classes, from first through

sixth grade. Like other schools for black children in the South, the Pine Level school did not have even the basic facilities that white schools did. Rosa's school was an old, one-room wooden building that was close to falling down. The schoolroom had no desks. Instead, students sat on long wooden benches in order of their age. The school had no windows and was brutally hot in the spring and summer. In the winter, an old wooden stove did its best to heat the room. After school, Rosa and the other students took their few books and papers home with them. They could not leave anything in the school because everyone was afraid that the Ku Klux

Klan might burn the building down during the night.

Sixth grade was the end of schooling for most black children in Alabama. In the entire state, there were only a couple of black junior high and high schools, and they were in the big cities.

When Rosa finished sixth grade, she wanted more education. Mrs. McCauley took her daughter to Montgomery, Alabama. There, the eleven-year-old enrolled at a private school called the Montgomery Industrial School for Girls, better known as Miss White's school. Alice White, who founded the school, came from Massachusetts. She and all her teachers were white. All the students were black. It was the first time that Rosa was treated as an equal by white people.

Miss White's school was private. The state did not support it in any way. Families who could afford to pay for their daughters' education did so. The rest of the money to run the school came from local churches and from Mr. Julius Rosenwald, a rich and generous man who believed in education for all people.

Mrs. McCauley paid for Rosa's first year at Miss White's school. After that, her daughter was awarded a full scholarship. She also worked at the school, cleaning blackboards, sweeping, and dusting to help pay her tuition. Rosa studied the usual school subjects, including English, science, arithmetic, and geography. The girls also learned sewing, cooking, and some nursing. Rosa lived with an aunt in Montgomery while she attended Miss White's school.

Life in Montgomery was very different than life in Pine Level. For one thing, it was much more segregated. Rosa and her brother were often confronted by bullying white children, angry adults, and storekeepers who would not wait on them. They had to follow Montgomery's strict segregation laws. They even had to drink out of "colored only" water fountains. Rosa was very upset by this unfair treatment, especially when her family told her not to fight back or confront anyone who bullied her. Her family had always told her that she was as good as anyone else. Her teachers at school told her the same thing. But Rosa soon learned that different rules applied to her, just because she was black.

After Rosa had finished eighth grade, the school closed. Miss White had grown too old to continue working. Rosa stayed in Montgomery and enrolled at Booker T. Washington Junior High School, where she completed ninth grade. Then she enrolled at the Alabama State Teachers' College for Negroes. This college trained black teachers. The students learned by teaching at a high school run by the college. Rosa attended this high school for tenth and part of eleventh grade.

CHAPTER 6:

Disappointment . . .
and Love

When Rosa was sixteen, Grandmother Edwards
got very sick, and Rosa had to leave school to take
care of her. Rosa's grandmother died a month
later. The teenager returned to Montgomery and

got a job in a shirt factory. This allowed Rosa to earn enough to live on while she went back to school. But then Mrs. McCauley became sick, and Rosa left school again to look after her mother.

Rosa missed school. She wanted to get her high school diploma and make something of herself. But family responsibilities came first. Rosa's job was to look after her mother and the house. Sometimes she cleaned houses or did sewing to make extra money. Sylvester worked as a carpenter and supported the family.

In 1931, a friend intro-
duced Rosa to Raymond
Parks. Everyone called
him Parks. He was a gen-
tle, hardworking barber
in Montgomery. At
first, Rosa was not
very interested in
Parks, but she soon
came to love and

admire him. They dated for two years and married on December 18, 1932. Rosa was almost twenty years old, and Parks was ten years older.

Raymond was a fine person in many ways. He encouraged his young wife to finish school, and Rosa graduated from Alabama Teacher's College in 1933. At home, he added to her education by sharing his knowledge and experience. Long before most people heard of civil rights, he was involved in the struggle for equality.

He was a member of the NAACP and was glad when his wife wanted to join the group. He believed in being a man and expected to be treated like a man, Rosa later wrote.

Times were hard for most Americans during the 1930s, especially for black people. Those were the years of the Great Depression. Millions of people were out of work. Rosa and Raymond Parks were lucky. Both of them had jobs. They didn't earn much, but they made enough with his barbering and her sewing to pay their bills.

CHAPTER 7:

Fighting for Justice

At the end of 1941, the United States entered World War II. Blacks and whites were drafted into the army to fight for their country. But blacks weren't treated equally. Bigots and racists everywhere felt that liberty and justice were the rights of white people only.

Rosa looked at the segregation all around her. She saw clearly that there was no liberty or justice for black people. She saw that there was a war to be fought at home: a peaceful war against injustice. For that reason, she became very active in the NAACP.

Rosa led a busy life. During the day, she worked at the Montgomery Fair department store. She

also earned money sewing at home and as a life-insurance agent.

Her evenings and weekends were often spent working as the secretary of the local NAACP chapter. She kept a record of membership dues. She wrote letters and information bulletins that were sent around the country to newspapers, radio stations, NAACP contributors, and members. She also kept records of crimes committed against black people. These stories made her very angry.

Rosa made sure that instances of discrimination and violence against blacks were recorded.
She kept track of legal cases, jailings, lynchings,
and other anti-black activities. All of this helped
prepare her for her own place in black history.
Then came that fateful day in December 1955,
and Rosa led the civil-rights movement into a
new era.

CHAPTER 8:
A Different Year

The bus boycott that followed Rosa's brave deed lasted just over a year. It was a very difficult year for everyone in Montgomery. Because black people continued the boycott, the bus company could not afford to run most of the buses anymore. This made the company very angry. Merchants were angry because without public transportation, fewer customers came downtown to shop in their stores. City officials were angry, too. They charged Rosa, Martin Luther King, Jr., and the other leaders of the boycott with breaking a law that said boycotts were illegal. Once again, Rosa was

arrested and fingerprinted. Her picture appeared in newspapers across the country.

Rosa was famous. The *New York Times* called her a "freedom fighter." She was invited to speak at schools, churches, and civil-rights meetings around the country. She met many famous people and was called an American hero.

Despite her fame, life at home was difficult. Rosa lost her job at the Montgomery Fair department store because of her civil-rights work and had to take in sewing at home to earn money. She and her husband and mother received death threats. Her husband was so worried about Rosa that he became very sick. Rosa's health suffered, too. Still she fought on. She knew that changing the laws of segregation was worth all the trouble and pain.

Finally, on November 13, 1956, the U.S. Supreme Court declared the Montgomery bus segregation laws unconstitutional. Martin Luther King, Jr. and the other boycott leaders urged everyone to stay off the buses until the written order from the Supreme Court was received in Montgomery. That day came on December 20. The boycott had lasted for one year and fifteen days. The next day, black people and white people rode the buses together, sitting wherever a seat was available.

The peaceful Montgomery bus boycott set an example that was followed throughout the South. Stores, lunch counters, bus stations, drinking fountains, restrooms, hospitals . . . one by one, they became equally available to people of all races.

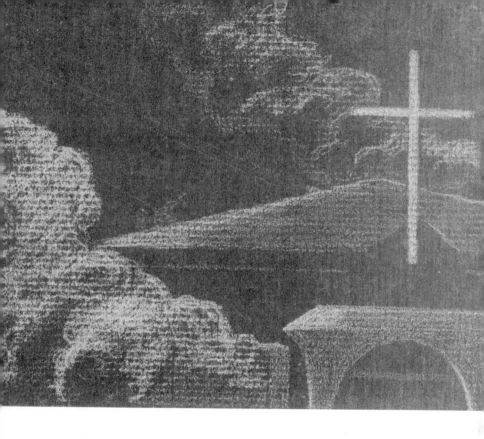

These victories didn't come easily. Churches were bombed, civil-rights workers — black and white — were beaten and murdered. Rosa was unable to find work in Alabama. She and her family continued to be threatened regularly. Raymond also was unable to find work, and Mrs. McCauley was ill. Finally, in August 1957, the family left Alabama and moved to Detroit,

Michigan. Rosa's brother, Sylvester McCauley, who had moved there years before, found an apartment for them to live in.

CHAPTER 9:
A Place in History

Rosa stayed active in the civil-rights movement. She also worked first as a receptionist, then as staff assistant to Representative John Conyers of Michigan. Congressman Conyers relied on Rosa to run his Detroit office while he was away in Washington, D.C. She spent much of her time recording the problems of the people in Conyers' district, many of whom were black. Then Conyers and his staff did their best to help these people find jobs, get health care, and fight discrimination. She remained in that job from 1965 through 1988.

Retirement wasn't the end of her life of service. In February 1987, she co-founded The Rosa and Raymond Parks Institute for Self-Development with her friend and secretary Elaine Eason Steele, in honor of Raymond Parks, who had died in 1977. The goal of the Institute was to provide education and guidance for young people. Rosa never forgot the sense of self-worth that molded her life. She wanted to pass on that quality to as many others as possible.

The Institute offered many programs to inner-city teens to help them obtain job and leadership skills. They learned to behave politely. They worked on their reading and writing skills. Most of all, they learned to reach out to the

community and help others improve their lives, too.

Every summer, the Institute took a busload of teenagers on a trip called "Pathways to Freedom." The teens visited important civil-rights sites all over the United States and Canada. Rosa wanted young people to understand the violent and painful history behind the freedoms they enjoyed. She also wanted

them to see how just one person could make a difference.

Many honors and words of praise were bestowed upon Rosa. She was the mother of the civil-rights movement, and words cannot do full justice to her accomplishments. But in Montgomery, Alabama, there is a special kind of monument that pleased Rosa very much. The bus on which she made history ran along Cleveland Avenue. Today, that street is called Rosa Parks Boulevard.

INDEX